Looking After Scotty

Written by Anna Porter

Illustrated by Steve Axelsen

Flying Start
to Literacy®

T0342934

Contents

Chapter 1: A dog called Scotty

Ethan and Ashley did not like Scotty. Scotty was the dog who lived in the house next door.

He dribbled everywhere. He chewed their toys and put them in holes that he dug in the yard. He never came when he was called.

And he was smelly!

One day Scotty's owner, Miss Brown, came to visit. Scotty looked very clean. He wagged his tail and he sat quietly.

Miss Brown said to Ethan and Ashley, "I need to visit my sister today, but I can't take Scotty with me. Would you look after him and take him for a walk in the park?"

Ethan and Ashley agreed to help.

Chapter 2: Run, Scotty, run!

As soon as Miss Brown left, Scotty grabbed Ashley's doll and started to rip it apart.

"Stop that, Scotty!" said Ashley.

When Ethan went to pull the doll away from Scotty, he snarled and ran out the door.

"Come back, Scotty!" yelled Ethan.

Ethan and Ashley ran after him.

Ethan and Ashley saw a hole under the fence.

Ethan said, "Oh, no! Scotty has dug his way out of the backyard. He has run away."

They raced down to the park, looking for Scotty. They called out for Scotty but he did not come back to them.

Then Ethan and Ashley saw Scotty running into the long grass. They ran into the long grass after him.

They got seeds from the grass all over their socks, but they did not catch Scotty.

Scotty ran into some creeping plants
that were growing near the creek.

Ethan and Ashley kept calling out
to Scotty but he did not come back.
They ran after him but they got
tangled up in the creepers.

"Scotty," they called. "Come back here!"

But Scotty did not come back.
He came out of the creepers
and ran away from them.

Chapter 3: Cleaning Scotty

Then Ashley spotted Scotty on the other side of the fence.

"There he is. He's in the prickly plants," she said, as they climbed over the fence and grabbed him.

"Ouch," said Ashley. "He has burrs, seeds and prickles all over his coat. And what's that sticky oily stuff on his ears and tail? Oh, yuck!"

Ethan and Ashley carried Scotty home.

Then they washed him with hot, soapy water. The seeds, prickles and burrs were stuck to Scotty's feet, ears and tail. As Ethan and Ashley pulled out the seeds, prickles and burrs, Scotty wriggled and snarled.

"He is a bad dog," said Ashley. "I hope Miss Brown comes back soon."

Chapter 4: Good boy, Scotty!

Soon Miss Brown came to pick up Scotty. He wagged his tail and licked her face.

Miss Brown said, "Oh, you have done such a good job looking after Scotty. He looks so beautiful and clean. But what happened to you?"

Ethan and Ashley looked at each other.

"We ran through some long grass and got tangled up in some creepers," said Ethan.

"And then we fell on some prickly plants," said Ashley.

"Well, you really must be more careful next time," said Miss Brown. "It's a good thing that Scotty didn't follow you!"

Chapter 5:
Oh no! Not again!

As Miss Brown was leaving, she said, "My sister wants me to go to her house for a week. Now that I know you can look after Scotty so well, maybe you could look after him for the whole week while I'm away!"

A note from the author

We once had a dog that loved to run away and get covered in all sorts of prickly and sticky plants and anything else she could roll in. I was always asking my young friends to help me look for her in the paddocks near our house or in the school ground as she loved to go and share the children's lunches with them. It was such a hard job to keep getting out all those prickles and burrs, and she was never happy having a bath to get clean again.